MATH IN OUR WORLD

USING MONEY
ON A SHOPPING TRIP

MIDLOTHIAN PUBLIC LIBRARY
14701 S. KENTON AVE.
MIDLOTHIAN, IL 60445

By Jennifer Marrewa
Photographs by Kay McKinley

Reading consultant: Susan Nations, M.Ed.,
author/literacy coach/consultant in literacy development
Math consultant: Rhea Stewart, M.A., mathematics content specialist

WEEKLY READER®
PUBLISHING

Please visit our web site at **www.garethstevens.com**
For a free color catalog describing our list of high-quality books,
call 1-800-542-2595 (USA) or 1-800-387-3178 (Canada). Our fax: 1-877-542-2596

Library of Congress Cataloging-in-Publication Data

Marrewa, Jennifer.
    Using money on a shopping trip / Jennifer Marrewa.
        p. cm. — (Math in our world. Level 2)
     ISBN-13: 978-0-8368-9004-4 (lib. bdg.)
     ISBN-10: 0-8368-9004-3 (lib. bdg.)
     ISBN 978-0-8368-9013-6 (softcover)
     ISBN-10: 0-8368-9013-2 (softcover)
     1. Counting—Juvenile literature. 2. Money—Juvenile literature. I. Title.
    QA113.M3653 2008
    513.2'11—dc22   2007033377

This edition first published in 2008 by
Weekly Reader® Books
An Imprint of Gareth Stevens Publishing
1 Reader's Digest Road
Pleasantville, NY 10570-7000 USA

Senior Editor: Brian Fitzgerald
Creative Director: Lisa Donovan
Graphic Designer: Alexandria Davis

Printed in the United States

1 2 3 4 5 6 7 8 9 10 09 08 07

TABLE OF CONTENTS

Words that appear in the glossary are printed in **boldface** type the first time they occur in the text.

Chapter 1:
Who Wants to Write?

There is a special visitor at school today. A writer talks to the class. He tells the children about the books he writes. He says that being an **author** is fun.

Von, Sara, and Jane love the stories the author shares. They want to write stories, too. They decide to start a writing club. They can make books together.

The next day they meet at Jane's house.
They talk about the stories they will write.
They talk about the pictures they will draw
for their stories.

The friends need some supplies to get started. Sara says they need pencils. Jane thinks they need a pink block **eraser.** Von says they need paper. He thinks a big **notebook** is best.

Chapter 2:
Time to Go Shopping

Von makes a list of the things they need to buy. The children put money in their pockets. They are ready to go to the store with Jane's mom.

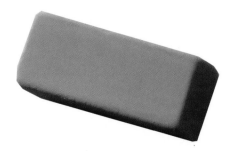

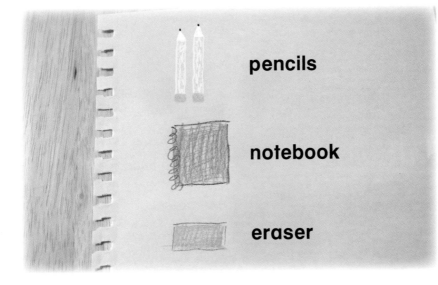

pencils

notebook

eraser

At the store the children look for the items they need to buy. Von takes the list out of his pocket. He reads the list again. Then he and the girls walk through the store to find the items.

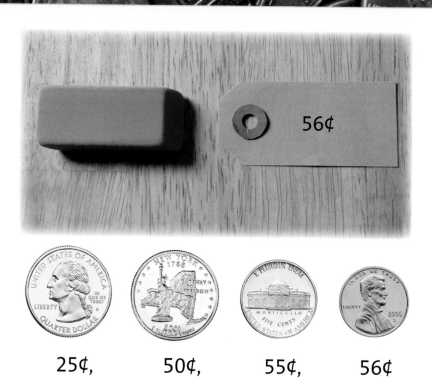

25¢,   50¢,   55¢,   56¢

They find a pink block eraser they want to buy. It costs 56¢. Jane has two quarters. Sara has a nickel. Von has a penny. This makes 56¢. They will use these coins to buy the eraser.

10¢,   20¢,   30¢,   31¢,   32¢

Sara finds the pencils. One box of pencils costs 32¢. Sara has three dimes. Von gives her a penny. This makes 31¢. Jane adds another penny. This makes 32¢. They will use these coins to buy the box of pencils.

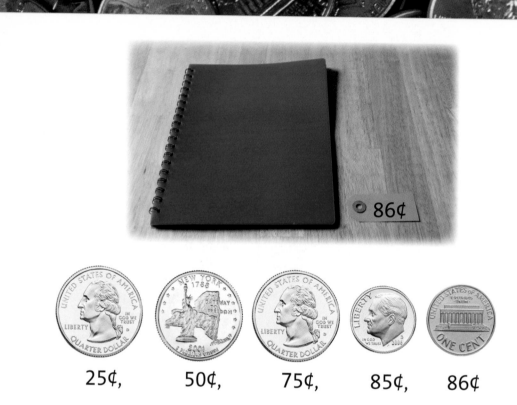

25¢,   50¢,   75¢,   85¢,   86¢

Von finds a big notebook. He wants the
notebook with the blue cover. It costs 86¢.
Von has three quarters. Sara has one dime.
Jane has one penny. This makes 86¢. They
will use these coins to buy the blue notebook.

They walk to the counter and pay for
their items. Now they have what they
need for their writing club. They also have
coins left over. Jane has a coin left in her
pocket. Sara and Von have coins left in
their pockets, too.

Chapter 3:
More Coins to Count!

The children look at their coins. Jane has one quarter left. Von also has one quarter left. Sara has one quarter and one dime left in her pocket.

25¢,   50¢,   75¢,   85¢

How much money do they have all together? Jane puts her quarter on the counter. Von puts his quarter on the counter. Sara adds her quarter and her dime. They have 85¢ in all!

Chapter 4:
More Things to Buy

The children can buy something else for their writing club. What should they buy? They think and talk. They each have an idea.

Von thinks they should buy a pack of
colored pencils. The pack of pencils costs 95¢.
The children look at their coins. They do not
have enough money to buy the colored pencils.

90¢

Sara thinks they should buy markers.
The price of the markers is 90¢. The children
look at their coins again. They do not have
enough money to buy the markers.

85¢

Jane thinks they should buy a box of crayons. The price of a box of crayons is 85¢. The children look at their coins one more time. They have enough money to buy the crayons.

The crayons will be perfect for drawing pictures. The children go to the counter again. They pay for the crayons. Now they have all the things they need.

They leave the store with their items.
They have a box of pencils. They have a pink
block eraser. They have a blue notebook
and a box of crayons.

The children talk on the way home. They
have lots of ideas for stories. They even think
about pictures.

Sara, Jane, and Von are ready to write. They write stories and draw pictures for their books. They are authors, just like the visitor who came to school.

Glossary

author: a person who writes books or stories

eraser: something used to rub out marks that are written or printed on paper

notebook: sheets of paper bound together like a book

About the Author

Jennifer Marrewa is a former elementary school teacher who writes children's books, poetry, nonfiction, and supplemental learning materials. She lives in California with her husband and two young children.